First World War
and Army of Occupation
War Diary
France, Belgium and Germany

2 DIVISION
19 Infantry Brigade
Royal Army Veterinary Corps
Veterinary Officer
21 August 1914 - 30 September 1914

WO95/1367/1

The Naval & Military Press Ltd
www.nmarchive.com
Published in association with The National Archives

Published by

The Naval & Military Press Ltd

Unit 10 Ridgewood Industrial Park,

Uckfield, East Sussex,

TN22 5QE England

Tel: +44 (0) 1825 749494

www.naval-military-press.com

www.nmarchive.com

This diary has been reprinted in facsimile from the original. Any imperfections are inevitably reproduced and the quality may fall short of modern type and cartographic standards.

© Crown Copyright
Images reproduced by permission of The National Archives, London, England, 2015.

Contents

Document type	Place/Title	Date From	Date To
Heading	WO95/1367 Vet Officer 19th Inf Bde		
Heading	Veterinary Officer. 1914 Aug To 1914 Sept. Brigade Train. Bde Ammunition Column Bde Supply Column. 1914 Aug To 1915 Aug.		
Heading	19th Infantry Brigade Veterinary Officer 19th Infantry Brigade August 1914		
Heading	Vety Officer 19th Infantry Brigade Volume I		
War Diary	Roven	21/08/1914	21/08/1914
War Diary	Amiens	22/08/1914	22/08/1914
War Diary	Valenciennes	22/08/1914	22/08/1914
War Diary	Blanc Missions	22/08/1914	23/08/1914
War Diary	Athur	24/08/1914	24/08/1914
War Diary	Rosin	24/08/1914	24/08/1914
War Diary	Presance	24/08/1914	24/08/1914
War Diary	Jeanbin	24/08/1914	25/08/1914
War Diary	Le Cateau	25/08/1914	26/08/1914
War Diary	L'Estroy	26/08/1914	27/08/1914
War Diary	Cugny	28/08/1914	28/08/1914
War Diary	Pontoise	28/08/1914	29/08/1914
War Diary	Carlepont	29/08/1914	30/08/1914
War Diary	Covboisy	30/08/1914	31/08/1914
War Diary	Kerbere	31/08/1914	31/08/1914
Heading	19th Infantry Brigade. Veterinary Officer 19th Infantry Brigade September 1914.		
Heading	V.O. i/c 19th Infantry Brigade Vol II 1-30.9.14		
War Diary	Verberie	01/09/1914	01/09/1914
War Diary	Dammartin	02/09/1914	02/09/1914
War Diary	Lagny	03/09/1914	04/09/1914
War Diary	Bria Comte Robert	05/09/1914	05/09/1914
War Diary	Grisy	05/09/1914	06/09/1914
War Diary	Gror to Fesres	06/09/1914	06/09/1914
War Diary	Villeneuve St Denis	07/09/1914	07/09/1914
War Diary	Villiers Sur Morin	08/09/1914	08/09/1914
War Diary	Pine Levce	09/09/1914	09/09/1914
War Diary	Near Commission	10/09/1914	10/09/1914
War Diary	Near Dmisty	10/09/1914	10/09/1914
War Diary	Chony	12/09/1914	12/09/1914
War Diary	Noyant	12/09/1914	14/09/1914
War Diary	Septmonts	14/09/1914	16/09/1914
War Diary	Venizel	16/09/1914	20/09/1914
War Diary	Septmonts	21/09/1914	30/09/1914
Miscellaneous	A Form. Messages And Signals.		
Miscellaneous	Messages And Signals.		
Miscellaneous	A Form. Messages And Signals.		

WO 95/13067

Net efficacy
rate by site

VETERINARY OFFICER.
1914 AUG TO 1914 SEPT.
BRIGADE TRAIN.
BDE AMMUNITION COLUMN.
BDE SUPPLY COLUMN.
1914 AUG TO 1915 AUG.

1367

VETERINARY OFFICER.
1914 AUG TO 1914 SEPT.

BRIGADE TRAIN.
BDE AMMUNITION COLUMN.
BDE SUPPLY COLUMN.
1914 AUG TO 1915 AUG.

19th Infantry Brigade

VETERINARY OFFICER

19th INFANTRY BRIGADE

AUGUST 1914.

12/966

WAR DIARY

Vety Officer. 19th Infantry Brigade

Volume I

Army Form C. 2118.

WAR DIARY
or
INTELLIGENCE SUMMARY.
(Erase heading not required.)

Instructions regarding War Diaries and Intelligence Summaries are contained in F. S. Regs., Part II. and the Staff Manual respectively. Title pages will be prepared in manuscript.

Hour, Date, Place	Summary of Events and Information	Remarks and references to Appendices
12.15 p.m. 21/8/14 Rouen	Received orders from Director of Veterinary Services, to proceed to Amiens at once and report to him there. Entrained with one charger at Gare du Nord.	
8.30 a.m. 22/8/14 — " —	Arrived Amiens, and reported to Base Commandant.	
4.35 a.m. 22/8/14 Amiens	Reported to D.V.S., & received orders from him to take over Veterinary charge of 19th Infantry Brigade & report myself to G.O.C. 19th Infantry Brigade.	
9.0. a.m. 22/8/14 — " —	Reported to G.O.C. 19th Infantry Brigade.	
10.15 a.m. 22/8/14 — " —	Received ord'rs as the went Veterinary Charts from O.C. No 7 Section Army Veterinary Corps.	
9. p.m. 22/8/14 — " —	Proceeded to guard the Park, and received one Field Veterinary Chest Officers. Entrained 22 horses belonging to Brigade Head Quarters. Shared in each truck. Instructions that no supplies from trip for the horses.	Ventilation of trucks very poor, doors had to be left open to obtain supplies from trip for the horses, stores had travelled well & no injuries occurred
6 a.m. 23/8/14 Valenciennes	Detrained.	
9.15 p.m. 23/8/14 — " —	Marched slowly on towards Belgian frontier on orders of General.	
4.35 p.m. 24/8/14 Blanc Misseron	Arrived at Blanc Misseron and were billeted for the night	Part of the horses had only arrived ... to supplement our ...
12.30. a.m. 23/8/14 — " —	Proceed Offr in Company with Supply Train	

Army Form C. 2118.

WAR DIARY
or
INTELLIGENCE SUMMARY.
(Erase heading not required.)

Instructions regarding War Diaries and Intelligence Summaries are contained in F. S. Regs., Part II. and the Staff Manual respectively. Title pages will be prepared in manuscript.

Hour, Date, Place	Summary of Events and Information	Remarks and references to Appendices
12.30 a.m. 23/8/14 Blero [Jurbise]	Marched all through the remainder of the hours of darkness without a halt.	
12 noon 24/8/14 Athis	Went on towards Athis, but were turned back & proceeded towards Pommeroeul.	
1. p.m. 24/8/14 Pommeroeul	to show signs of distress so a halt for 1 hour was called. All horses were watered and fed. The pace had been fast & the road very hilly, consequently several of the horses had cast shoes & were showing symptoms of exhaustion.	The village of Pommeroeul was probably being used as a large measure to the fact that a great many of them were & yet & had not been washed regularly up to date.
2 p.m. 24/8/14	Moved on & passed through Villers Pol to Preux where a short halt to water & feed was called.	
4.15 p.m. 24/8/14 Preux	Moved off & arrived at Taisnières just before	
7.15 p.m. 24/8/14 Taisnières	Nightfall. Billetted for the night.	
4. a.m. 25/8/14	Two of the horses belonging to the Reserve Ammunition Column were unable to move & were forthwith destroyed as we had to return speedily. One of them cases was dumnitis & the other a very bad kick received the day before, during the backing point open.	All else being recorded asleep in the night.
5. a.m. 25/8/14	Moved off with Brigade Headquarters.	
7 p.m. 25/8/14 Le Câteau	Proceeded all day tomorrow to Le Câteau. Arrived at Le Câteau & billetted there the night.	

WAR DIARY
or
INTELLIGENCE SUMMARY.
(Erase heading not required.)

Army Form C. 2118.

Instructions regarding War Diaries and Intelligence Summaries are contained in F. S. Regs., Part II. and the Staff Manual respectively. Title pages will be prepared in manuscript.

Hour, Date, Place	Summary of Events and Information	Remarks and references to Appendices
9 p.m. 25/8/14 Le Cateau	A draught horse belonging to the train was shot probably to a battery.	Order in the area was probably to a battery. No. 9.0. or No. 1 mobile.
11 p.m. 25/8/14	Orders received round about 3rd regiment cavalry became very insistent and that	
6 a.m. 26/8/14	Retired very hurriedly as the enemy were entering the town, remained with Brigade Headquarters	
7.15 a.m. 26/8/14	The Brigade took up position on connection with the 5th Division on the battlefield between La Catrau & Reumont. Water was obtainable for the horses, and there was oat hay in abundance on the fields.	Horses were given a quantity of oat hay as oat hay was absolutely a necessity.
5.15 p.m. 26/8/14	Further retreat after the battle. It was impossible to keep touch with Headquarters of the Brigade and retreated with the remainder of the units. At Reumont to St Quentin. Came up with some of the Brigade & remained near the Brigade Field Ambulance.	
9 p.m. 26/8/14 J.Estrig		
4 a.m. 27/8/14	Moved off in company with the 14th Brigade Field Ambulance thro' St Quentin and thence	
6 p.m. 27/8/14	Bivouacked near Cugny. The horses that were there were impressed by the Middlesex regiment. First line of Transport was destroyed as they were very badly gulled & quite exhausted.	Horse harness had not been off for nearly 3 days. Men exhausted from want of sleep. No

Army Form C. 2118.

WAR DIARY
or
INTELLIGENCE SUMMARY.
(Erase heading not required.)

Instructions regarding War Diaries and Intelligence Summaries are contained in F.S. Regs., Part II. and the Staff Manual respectively. Title pages will be prepared in manuscript.

Hour, Date, Place	Summary of Events and Information	Remarks and references to Appendices
10 a.m. 28.8.14 Cugny	Moved off & passed thro' Cugny, Bahincourt, Noyon to Pontoise. The roads for the most part were macadam & very bad travelling for the horses.	The horses slipped a good deal on the greasy roads.
6 p.m. 28.8.14 Pontoise	Arrived & billeted.	
11 a.m. 29.8.14 Pontoise	Inspected all the horses and found that 30 percent of the horses were really unfit for immediate work, but as there was nothing for it and no possible chance to evacuate the sick and in any case no possibility to replace them.	Several of these horses were badly galled, but if they had one day's rest they were serviceable again for a rapid recovery.
8 p.m. 29.8.14 —	Moved off in company with the baggage train.	
11 p.m. 29.8.14 Coulofort	Arrived at Coulofort & bivouacked for the night.	
3 a.m. 30.8.14 Coulofort	Moved off & proceeded at a slow pace halted twice & fed at regular intervals.	Roads in good order for travelling.
5.30 p.m. 30.8.14 Conlorty	Arrived at Conlorty.	
6 a.m. 31.8.14 Conlorty	Moved off & proceeded as on the previous day at a good cadence with regular halts & food & water.	
7.15 p.m. 31.8.14 Kerbine	Arrived and bivouacked for the night.	

F. F. Gourion Lieut.
V.O. & C. 9th Infantry Brigade

19th Infantry Brigade.

VETERINARY OFFICER

19th INFANTRY BRIGADE

SEPTEMBER 1914.

VI

121/1084

I.O. 1/c 19th Infantry Brigade

Vol II — 1-30.9.14

Army Form C. 2118.

WAR DIARY
or
INTELLIGENCE SUMMARY.
(Erase heading not required.)

Instructions regarding War Diaries and Intelligence Summaries are contained in F. S. Regs., Part II. and the Staff Manual respectively. Title pages will be prepared in manuscript.

Hour, Date, Place	Summary of Events and Information	Remarks and references to Appendices

Army Form C. 2118.

WAR DIARY
or
INTELLIGENCE SUMMARY

(Erase heading not required.)

Instructions regarding War Diaries and Intelligence Summaries are contained in F. S. Regs., Part II, and the Staff Manual respectively. Title pages will be prepared in manuscript.

Hour, Date, Place	Summary of Events and Information	Remarks and references to Appendices
10 a.m. 6 9 10 Bivouac	moved off	
10.45 a.m. 6/9/14 Gorsy	halted and watered	
	Reported numbers of sick to Brigade full on repts [?]	
	[illegible] ahead for two hours [?]	
	Returning [illegible]	
6.30 a.m. 8/9/14	[illegible] of [illegible] from —	
12 noon 8/9/14 Bois de Cuspins	Halted watered & fed & [illegible]	
10.15	moved on	
12 midnight Villemoine (?) [illegible]	Arrived & Bivouaced	
6 a.m. 7/9/14	moved on but Town road slowly all day & halted	
	to water & feed at regular intervals.	
6 p.m. — 7/9/14 Villeneuve-sur-Morin	Halted on farm & stayed night & [illegible] cavalry	
	no orders to move received	

WAR DIARY
or
INTELLIGENCE SUMMARY.
(Erase heading not required.)

Army Form C. 2118.

Instructions regarding War Diaries and Intelligence Summaries are contained in F. S. Regs., Part II. and the Staff Manual respectively. Title pages will be prepared in manuscript.

III

Hour, Date, Place	Summary of Events and Information	Remarks and references to Appendices
6.0 p.m. 8.9.14 Villiers-sur-Marne	Bivouacked. Through heavy rain and squalls of wind.	
12 noon - in Pierre Levée	Bivouaced. Rested all day.	
9.9.14 Pierre Levée	Prepared in Bivouac all day	Purchased my horse & groom's horse. All of which were necessary.
9.30 p.m.	Moved off. Road crowded all night.	
10.15-0.m. 10.9.14 Aux Coulommiers	Turned into a field to Bivouac.	Handed over 10 horses bought to procure further. To O.C. 20th Ammunition.
2 p.m. - " -	Moved off through La Ferté, crossing the Marne by Pontoon Bridge without incident.	
8.0 a.m 10.9.14 Rear Doirny	Bivouaced in a field, where there was no water at hand. Horses had to be taken a distance of 3 miles to water.	Destroyed my own charger which had been kicked the day before & very badly wounded in pasture.
10.15 a.m. 11.9.14 - " -	Moved off & marched all day with one short halt at 4 p.m. and on again all night.	
1.30 a.m. 12.9.14 Chévry	Arrived. Halted watered and fed.	Provided very bad, as result of heavy rain all day. Also very bad by roads to bog & boggy.

Army Form C. 2118.

WAR DIARY
or
INTELLIGENCE SUMMARY.
(Erase heading not required.)

Hour, Date, Place	Summary of Events and Information	Remarks and references to Appendices
2 p.m. 12.9.14 Chouy.	Moved off and marched MB on in HS8 the direction of Soissons. Heavy rain all the time.	Roads very bad owing to rain. Troops cheering very cheerful.
8 p.m. 12.9.14. Roganh.	Halted on the main Soissons road.	Some very bad hills.
13.9.14. "	Stayed in same position all day, but subsequently moved & turned out into a field to graze.	No hay.
10.15 a.m 14.9.14	Moved off.	
11 a.m " Septmont	Arrived and halted in the village	
9 p.m " "	Moved off with supply waggons.	
11 p.m " Venizel	Reported Brigade Headquarters. Reported to G.O.C. 19th Brigade	Handed over one horse to O.C. 2nd Battalion.
9 a.m 15 Sep 14. "	[struck through]	Plenty of good water with in easy reach. Hay drawn locally for horses.
16.9.14, 17.9.14, 18.9.14	Inspected unit with a view to having worn off materiel store up inspected cobs.	
19.9.14 Venizel.	No change in position. Daily dosing of all cases without result.	Destroyed one little one. Commencing sore back

Army Form C. 2118.

WAR DIARY
or
INTELLIGENCE SUMMARY.
(Erase heading not required.)

V

Instructions regarding War Diaries and Intelligence Summaries are contained in F.S. Regs., Part II. and the Staff Manual respectively. Title pages will be prepared in manuscript.

Hour, Date, Place	Summary of Events and Information	Remarks and references to Appendices
8 p.m. 20.9.14 Kenyel	Returned to Teplemouth	
10.15 p.m. Teplemouth	Arrived and went into Billets	
21.9.14 — " —	Received 64 Remounts from Rail head & distributed them to various units of Brigade.	Another purchase of hay locally from
22.9.14 — " —	Handed over 21 Horses to O.C. No H Mobile Veterinary Section. Inspected all units & reflected all cases.	All cases handed over to O.C. No H Mobile Section were inspected
23.9.14 — " —	Handed over 8 Horses to O.C. No H Mobile Veterinary Section.	& offered unrest & destroyed
24.9.14 — " —	Received 8 heavy draught remounts from rail head and distributed them to units of Brigade.	all cases
25.9.14 — " —	Handed over 4 Horses to O.C. No H Mobile Veterinary Section. Received 2 heavy draught remounts handed them to Middlesex Yeo.	Duty
26.9.14 — " —	Handed over 3 Horses to O.C. No H Mobile Veterinary Section.	

(9 29 6) W 3332—1107 100,000 10/13 H W V Forms/C. 2118/10.

WAR DIARY
or
INTELLIGENCE SUMMARY.
(Erase heading not required.)

Army Form C. 2118.

Hour, Date, Place	Summary of Events and Information	Remarks and references to Appendices
27.9.14. Septmoncel	Remained at Septmoncel. Early inspections made of all mounts and supervision of shoeing of all mounted.	Plenty of good water close at hand. Large amount of good grazing, all debilitated horses turned out to graze daily. Most of horses tethered up out of doors. Some horses in stable covers, mostly in French stables.
28.9.14. — " —	No change in affairs.	
29.9.14. — " —	Started out at 9.45 a.m. with Brigade requisitioning officer to purchase locally; two light waggons and purchased him battalion; for the purpose of carrying blankets & great coats during the winter months. Sixteen heavy draught horses in good condition and sound were purchased. All examined and passed by me. Brigade horses inspected by Colonel Butler, A.V.C.; everything satisfactory. Destroyed one case of Colic belonging to Ammunition Column. The animal had been in pain for nearly 24 hours & had proven no improvement and was in fact in an exhausted condition I considered that it was considered better to destroy him.	All units engaged in shoeing horses, hot, as there is a very useful local forge with two forges, in the village
30.9.14.	Septmoncel 30.9.14.	

H.E. Irwin Hunt
A.V.C.
V.O./c 19th Infantry Brigade

MESSAGES AND SIGNALS.

Army Form C. 2121.

TO: Officer Commanding Number Two Mobile Veterinary Section LANDRECIES

Sender's Number: V18
Day of Month: Twenty first
AAA

Please proceed HAUTMONT on twenty second for casualties first Division and despatch to BASE VETERINARY HOSPITAL ROUEN AAA repeat VET. First Division AAA Base Veterinary Hospital should always be notified of despatch of casualties.

From: VET
Place: Amiens
Time: 9.30

MESSAGES AND SIGNALS.

TO Officer Commanding No 7 Mobile Veterinary Section AULNOYE

Sender's Number: V 19
Day of Month: Twentyfirst
In reply to Number: 1
AAA

Please despatch casualties to Advanced Base Veterinary Hospital Amiens reporting despatch to Officer Commanding Hospital

From: VET
Place: Amiens
Time: 11.45 am

J Moore B Genl
ADVS

MESSAGES AND SIGNALS.

Prefix	Code	m.	Words	Charge	This message is on a/c of:	Recd. at	m.
Office of Origin and Service Instructions.			Sent			Date	
			At	m.	Service.	From	
			To		(Signature of "Franking Officer.")	By	
			By				

TO Base Commandant HAVRE

Sender's Number.	Day of Month	In reply to Number	AAA
V 20	Twenty first		

re my V15 number Seven ~~whose~~ Veterinary Section can now proceed AMIENS as soon as possible AAA repeat Deputy Director of Vety Services at HAVRE Offig Officer Commandg 7st_p should report Base Commandant AMIENS on arrival

From **VET**
Place **Amiens**
Time

Signature of Addressor: J Moore

MESSAGES AND SIGNALS.

TO: Officer Commanding No 2 Mobile Veterinary Section LANDRECIES

Sender's Number: V 21
Day of Month: Twenty first
AAA

Reference my V18 casualties first division can now be despatched to Advanced Base Veterinary Hospital AMIENS instead of ROUEN

From: VET
Place: AMIENS
Time: 12 noon

MESSAGES AND SIGNALS.

TO Deputy Director Vety Services HAVRE

Sender's Number: V.22
Day of Month: Twenty first
AAA

Please proceed General Headquarters as soon as you can reporting to me first

From: VET
Place: AMIENS
Time: 3 PM

MESSAGES AND SIGNALS.

TO: Officer Commanding Base Veterinary Hospital ROUEN

Sender's Number: V23
Day of Month: Twenty first
AAA

Wire time Lieut IRWIN expected to arrive AMIENS AAA very urgent stop He should bring one officers chest and one unit chest

From: VET
Place: Amiens
Time: 3.30 Pm

J Moore Brig Genl
D.V.S.

MESSAGES AND SIGNALS.

TO Assistant Director of Veterinary Serv
No. 1 Division

Sender's Number: V.24
Day of Month: Twenty-first

AAA

Advanced Base Veterinary Hospital opened at AMIENS AAA Detrainment at GARE SAN ROCH

From: VET.
Place: AMIENS

DVS

MESSAGES AND SIGNALS.

TO: Assistant Director of Veterinary Services No. 2 Division

Sender's Number: Y 25
Day of Month: Twenty first
AAA

Advanced Base Veterinary Hospital opened at AMIENS AAA Detachment at GARE SAN ROCH

From: VET
Place: AMIENS

DVS

"A" Form. Army Form C. 2121.
MESSAGES AND SIGNALS. No. of Message_____

Prefix____ Code____ m.	Words	Charge	This message is on a/c of:	Recd. at____ m.
Office of Origin and Service Instructions.	Sent			Date_____
	At____ m.		_____Service.	From_____
	To			
	By		(Signature of "Franking Officer.")	By

TO { Assistant Director of Veterinary Services
No. 3 DIVISION

| Sender's Number | Day of Month | In reply to Number | AAA |
| V 26 | Twenty first | | |

Opened at | Advanced Base | Veterinary Hospital |
at | GARE | AMIENS SAN | AND Detrainment ROCH

From: VET.
Place: AMIENS
Time:

The above may be forwarded as now corrected. (Z)

Censor.   Signature of Addressor or person authorised to telegraph in his name.
* This line should be erased if not required.

"A" Form.　　　　　　　　　　Army Form C. 2121.
MESSAGES AND SIGNALS.　　　No. of Message

Prefix	Code	m.	Words	Charge	This message is on a/c of:	Recd. at	m.
			Sent			Date	
Office of Origin and Service Instructions.			At	m.	Service.	From	
			To				
			By		(Signature of "Franking Officer.")	By	

TO: Assistant Director of Veterinary Services
No 5 DIVISION

| Sender's Number | Day of Month | In reply to Number | |
| V.27 | Twenty first | | AAA |

Advanced Base Veterinary Hospital opened at GARE AMIENS SAN ROCH AAA Detrainment

From: VET.
Place: AMIENS
Time:

"A" Form.
Army Form C. 2121.
MESSAGES AND SIGNALS.   No. of Message_____

Prefix ___ Code ___ m.	Words	Charge	This message is on a/c of:	Recd. at ___ m.
Office of Origin and Service Instructions.				Date ___
	Sent		___ Service.	From ___
	At ___ m.			
	To			
___	By ___		(Signature of "Franking Officer.")	By ___

TO Officer Commanding
    No 1 Mobile Veterinary Section
    RAILHEAD

| Sender's Number | Day of Month | In reply to Number | AAA |
| V. 78 | Twenty first | | |

opened Advanced Base Veterinary Hospital
at   at   AMIENS   AAA Detrainment
        GARE   SAN   ROCH.

From VET.
Place AMIENS
Time

"A" Form.
MESSAGES AND SIGNALS.
Army Form C. 2121.
No. of Message _____

| Prefix ___ Code ___ m. | Words | Charge | This message is on a/c of: | Recd. at ___ m. |
| Office of Origin and Service Instructions. | Sent At ___ m. To By | | ___ Service. (Signature of "Franking Officer.") | Date ___ From ___ By |

TO: Officer Commanding
No. 2 Mobile Veterinary Section
RAILHEAD

Sender's Number	Day of Month	In reply to Number	
V 29	Twenty first		AAA

Opened at Advanced Base Veterinary Hospital at GARE AMIENS AAA Detachment SAN ROCH

From: VET.
Place: AMIENS
Time:

The above may be forwarded as now corrected. (Z)

Censor. Signature of Addressee or person authorised to telegraph in his name.
* This line should be erased if not required.

"A" Form.   Army Form C. 2121.
MESSAGES AND SIGNALS.   No. of Message..........

Prefix......Code......m.	Words	Charge	This message is on a/c of:	Recd. at..........m.
Office of Origin and Service Instructions.	Sent		..........Service.	Date..........
....	At..........m.			From..........
....	To..........		(Signature of "Franking Officer.")	By..........
	By..........			

TO { Officer Commanding
     No 3 Mobile Veterinary Section
     RAILHEAD

| Sender's Number | Day of Month | In reply to Number | AAA |
| V 30 | Twenty four | | |

Advanced Base Veterinary Hospital opened at GARE AMIENS SAN AAA Detrainment ROCH

From VET.
Place AMIENS
Time

The above may be forwarded as now corrected.   (Z)

Censor.   Signature of Addressor or person authorised to telegraph in his name.
* This line should be erased if not required.

"A" Form.
Army Form C. 2121.
MESSAGES AND SIGNALS.

TO: Officer Commanding No. 4 Mobile Veterinary Section RAILHEAD

Sender's Number: V.31
Day of Month: Twenty first

Advanced Base Veterinary Hospital opened at AMIENS AAA Detachment at GARE SAN ROCH

From: VET.
Place: AMIENS

"A" Form.
MESSAGES AND SIGNALS.
Army Form C. 2121.

TO: Officer Commanding No 5 Mobile Veterinary Section RAILHEAD

Sender's Number: V.32
Day of Month: Twenty first

Opened at Advanced Base Veterinary Hospital at AMIENS GARE SAN ROCH AAA Detrainment

From: VET
Place: AMIENS

"A" Form.
MESSAGES AND SIGNALS.
Army Form C. 2121.
No. of Message _____

Prefix ___ Code ___ m.	Words	Charge	This message is on a/c of:	Recd. at ___ m.
Office of Origin and Service Instructions.	Sent			Date
	At ___ m.		___ Service.	From
	To			
	By		(Signature of "Franking Officer.")	By

TO: Officer Commanding
No. 7 Mobile Veterinary Section
RAILHEAD

Sender's Number	Day of Month	In reply to Number	
V.33	Twenty first		AAA

Advanced Base Veterinary Hospital opened at AMIENS AAA Detrainment at GARE SAN ROCH

From: VET.
Place: AMIENS
Time:

"A" Form.
MESSAGES AND SIGNALS.
Army Form C. 2121.

TO: Officer Commanding
No 8 Mobile Veterinary Section
RAILHEAD

Sender's Number: V 34
Day of Month: Twenty first

AAA

Advanced Base Veterinary Hospital opened at AMIENS AAA Detachment at GARE SAN ROCH

From: VET
Place: AMIENS

"A" Form.
Army Form C. 2121.
MESSAGES AND SIGNALS.

TO: Officer Commanding No. 9 Mobile Veterinary Section RAILHEAD

Sender's Number: V.35
Day of Month: Twenty First
AAA

Advanced Base Veterinary Hospital opened at AMIENS and Detrainment at GARE SAN ROCH

From: VET
Place: AMIENS

"A" Form.   Army Form C. 2121.
MESSAGES AND SIGNALS.   No. of Message_____

TO	Officer Commanding No 10 Mobile Veterinary Section RAILHEAD

Sender's Number	Day of Month	In reply to Number	
V.36	Twenty first		AAA

Advanced Base Veterinary Hospital opened at AMIENS AAA Detachment at GARE SAN ROCH.

From: VET.
Place: AMIENS
Time:

"A" Form. Army Form C. 2121.
MESSAGES AND SIGNALS.

TO: Assistant Director of Veterinary Services
Cavalry Division

Sender's Number: V.37
Day of Month: Twenty first

AAA

Advanced Base Veterinary Hospital opened at AMIENS AAA Detachment at GARE SAN ROCH

From: VET.
Place: AMIENS

DVS

"A" Form.
Army Form. C. 2121.
MESSAGES AND SIGNALS.

| TO | General Haig First Army Corps |

Sender's Number	Day of Month	In reply to Number	AAA
V 38	Twenty second	G 40	

much regret cannot take Captain MOSLEY away from Command of his ~~~~ Veterinary Section but have detailed Captain O'RORKE who is most capable AAA in addition to executive duties can you ~~to~~ use him as intermediary in Veterinary matters between ~~for~~ HQ first Army corps and the Assistant Director Veterinary Services of First and second Divisions

From: Director Vety Services
Place: AMIENS
Time:

Signature: J Moore BG ~~DVS~~

"A" Form. Army Form C. 2121.
MESSAGES AND SIGNALS.

TO BASE COMMANDANT HARVE

Sender's Number	Day of Month	In reply to Number	AAA
V 39	Twenty second		

Please instruct Captain O'RORKE number two Veterinary Section to proceed as soon as possible to Head quarters first Army Corps for duty AAA repeat to Officer Commanding BASE Veterinary Hospital HARVE asking him to report departure to me

From VET
Place AMIENS
Time 8.45

Moore Bg

www.ingramcontent.com/pod-product-compliance
Lightning Source LLC
Chambersburg PA
CBHW081459160426
43193CB00013B/2535